YOU ARE
NOT ALONE

A Reflection Journal for Women Reclaiming
Themselves after Loss, Pain & Motherhood's
heavy seasons.

By: Erika Santiago
A Woman Who Sees You

ISBN: 979-8-218-81111-2

Published by She Is More Co.

Printed in the United States of America

Cover design by She Is More Co.

For disclaimer and guidance notes, please see page 4.

For information, contact:
🌐 www.payhip.com/SheIsMoreCo
✉ Esanti82123@gmail.com

Disclaimer

This journal is a companion, not a cure. It was created from my heart and lived experience — not from clinical expertise.

I am not a licensed therapist, counselor, or medical professional. The reflections, prompts, and affirmations shared within these pages are intended to support, not replace, professional mental health care.

If you are struggling with overwhelming emotions, trauma, or mental health challenges, I gently encourage you to seek support from a qualified professional. You deserve care that meets you fully.

This is your space — for reflection, softness, truth-telling, and healing at your own pace. Take what you need. Leave what you don't.

You are not alone.

About the Author

I'm a mother. A woman who knows what it feels like to disappear inside her own life.

This is the first thing I've ever written — not because I saw myself as a writer, but because I needed somewhere to be honest. Somewhere to pour the pain I was carrying, the truth I couldn't say out loud, and the healing I didn't yet understand.

This journal came from the quiet moments: after the kids were asleep, after the world stopped asking for more. I started writing not with answers, but with an ache. Somewhere in those pages, I began remembering who I was.

There were nights I cried quietly after everyone else had been cared for. Days when I held everything together but couldn't remember the last time I felt like myself. I didn't write this from a place of knowing — I wrote it from the middle of the mess. The becoming. The return.

I created You Are Not Alone for the woman I used to be... and maybe for the woman you are right now.

If these pages end up giving you space to breathe, or remind you of your softness, your voice, your strength — I would be honored to hear your story.

✉ You can reach me at: Esanti82123@gmail.com

You are not alone.
Not in your grief.
Not in your becoming.
Not ever.

TABLE OF CONTENTS
"A gentle guide through your healing"

TABLE OF CONTENTS
"A gentle guide through your healing"

Reflections (Continued)

TABLE OF CONTENTS
"A gentle guide through your healing"

Final Pages

Welcome To
You Are Not Alone

You don't have to be fully healed to begin.
You don't even have to be ready.
You just have to be here.

This journal was made for the woman holding everything together in silence — the one carrying grief, motherhood, pain, and pressure in her chest like a secret weight.
If that's you, know this: you are not alone.

Within these pages, you will not be asked to fix yourself.
You will be invited to meet yourself — gently, honestly, and without shame.

You will reflect.
You will write.
You will rest between the lines.

You'll find affirmations that hold space for your softness and prompts that ask you to look inward, not for judgment, but for truth.
Some days, you may only read.
Some days, you may cry.
Some days, you may write two words and still be doing the quiet work of returning to yourself.

There is no pace you must follow.
No perfect way to move through this.

There is only this page, this breath, this moment — and your voice.

Welcome home.

To the Woman Holding This Journal,

I want to begin by saying: I see you.

Not the polished version. Not the one powering through. I see the part of you that's tired — from holding it all together, from grieving in silence, from always being everything to everyone.

I wrote this journal because I was her too. The woman who smiled while breaking inside. The mother who poured so much into everyone else she forgot what it felt like to belong to herself. The woman who longed to be held, but only knew how to hold.

This isn't a self-help book. It's not a quick fix. It's a quiet return — a gathering of all the pieces of you that got lost along the way. These pages were born from my own becoming — not in bright breakthroughs, but in the quiet moments. In the weeping. In the numbness. In the stillness between who I was and who I was remembering myself to be.

You don't have to be okay to be worthy of healing. You don't have to know where you're going to begin.

You just have to start.

With one truth. One pause. One page. That's how I started, too.

Let this be your space to lay it all down — the grief, the rage, the tenderness, the questions. Let this be your reminder that softness is not weakness. That your story matters. That you're allowed to want more.

You are not alone in this.

With all my heart,
Erika
A woman who sees you

PREPARING FOR REFLECTION

Before you begin,take a moment for yourself. These reflections are raw, honest, and they deserve your full heart. You are safe to feel, pause, and return to yourself here.

GENTLE PROMPTS TO BEGIN YOUR REFLECTION

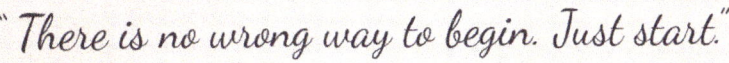

"There is no wrong way to begin. Just start."

As you begin this journey, take a deep breath. In one word, how are you truly feeling in this moment?

_____

_____

_____

_____

_____

_____

_____

_____

_____

_____

_____

Your healing, your story, your voice–its safe here

GENTLE PROMPTS TO BEGIN YOUR REFLECTION

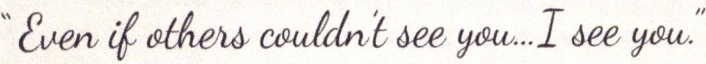

"Even if others couldn't see you...I see you."

When was the last time you truly felt seen, heard, or cared for?

_____

_____

_____

_____

_____

_____

_____

_____

_____

_____

_____

_____

_____

Your healing, your story, your voice–its safe here

GENTLE PROMPTS TO BEGIN YOUR REFLECTION

"She's still in me — waiting, not gone."

What version of yourself have you been missing — and how can you reconnect with her gently?

_____

_____

_____

_____

_____

_____

_____

_____

_____

_____

_____

_____

_____

GENTLE PROMPTS TO BEGIN YOUR REFLECTION

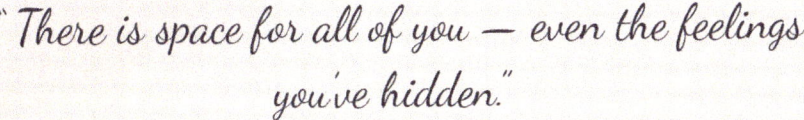

"There is space for all of you — even the feelings you've hidden."

What emotions have you been holding in silence— and how can you begin to release them?

_____

_____

_____

_____

_____

_____

_____

_____

_____

_____

_____

_____

_____

Your healing, your story, your voice-its safe here

I DON'T JUST
SURVIVE–
I RISE, I HEAL,
I LIVE

Reflection 1
"The Day I Got Tired of Being Tired"

There wasn't a single moment that made me realize I had lost myself. It wasn't loud or dramatic. It was quiet—like a slow undoing.

Grief consumed me after I lost my dad—the one person who had always made me feel safe. But even in my pain, life kept demanding more. I was nursing my baby, caring for my child with special needs, trying to give my middle child my attention, so he wouldn't feel left out. All while Surviving a relationship that drained more from me than it gave.

I was pouring into everyone, yet no one was pouring into me.

I remember crying in the bathroom most days—alone. I'd let the tears fall as silently as I could, then wipe my face, take a deep breath, and go back to being everything for everyone.

There was no applause.
No comfort.
No witness to my pain.

Just me, trying to survive.

And then one day, after another conversation that left me hollow, I knew: I could change everything about myself and it still wouldn't be enough—for him, for this life, for what I thought I had to be. I had been molding myself into what someone else wanted... and in doing that, I had disappeared.

That was the beginning.

I started turning to prayer, to scripture, to the small voice inside me that said, "this isn't how your story has to end." I realized I couldn't keep living like this—not just for me, but for my kids. They deserve the healthiest version of me, and so do I.

This is me choosing to rise—not in some grand, dramatic way, but in the soft, sacred act of showing up for myself again.

Undoing took time.
So did rising.
But this—this quiet return to myself—is how I begin again.

Reflection 1
Journal Prompts

"Exhaustion may have brought you here, but grace will carry you forward"

What moment made you realize you were running on empty — and still giving?

_____

_____

_____

_____

_____

_____

_____

_____

_____

_____

_____

_____

_____

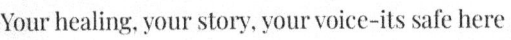
Your healing, your story, your voice–its safe here

Reflection 1
Journal Prompts

"Getting tired isn't weakness — it's your soul calling you back to you."

What part of you have you been silencing to keep upfloat?

_____

_____

_____

_____

_____

_____

_____

_____

_____

_____

_____

_____

_____

_____

Your healing, your story, your voice-its safe here

Reflection 1
Journal Prompts

"Your exhaustion is valid. Your healing is possible. Your return to yourself has already begun."

When you close your eyes and picture peace, what does it look like?

_____

_____

_____

_____

_____

_____

_____

_____

_____

_____

_____

_____

_____

_____

Your healing, your story, your voice–its safe here

Reflection 2

"I was a woman first."

I didn't have the luxury of getting to know myself as a woman before I became a mother. I was 18 when I had my first son—still growing, still discovering who I was. Yet, even in those early years, I felt strong. I worked, saved, showed up fully for my child. I still made space for family, friends, laughter, and moments that only belonged to me. I was confident, driven, and alive in my own skin.

But life kept asking more of me.

After my son's first birthday, he began having seizures. We were in and out of hospitals constantly. At times, I found it hard to keep a job because of all the emergencies my son had. Years later, when he turned eleven, everything shifted again—he stopped walking and eating. We spent weeks in the hospital. I was torn between being there for him and trying to be present for my one-year-old at home. I was drowning in mom guilt, bills, uncertainty... and even though I had support from a few close friends and family, I still felt like I was carrying it all on my own.

I lost my job.
I lost my rhythm.
And somewhere in the middle of it all—I lost myself.

I thought I found love again, but instead, I found more hurt. I gave everything I had to a man who, at that time, couldn't fully see me. I kept shrinking, quieting myself to keep the peace, slowly fading into someone I barely recognized. And then, just when I thought I had nothing left to lose, I lost my father—my anchor.

That grief shattered me into pieces.

After that, I stopped seeing myself as a woman. I became roles: a mother, partner, and caregiver. Someone who gave endlessly and didn't know how to ask for anything. I held all my grief behind closed doors—smiling in the day, falling apart in the dark.

Gently, quietly, I began to return to myself.
It started with a prayer. A cup of coffee in the morning, a clean face. A moment to breathe. A soft outfit that made me feel good, even if I had no where to go. A whispered reminder in the stillness: You are still in there.

One small choice at a time, I've begun remembering:
I am more than what I do for others.
More than the roles I carry.
More than a caretaker.
I am still a woman.

Let me remind you, too:

You were a woman first.
Motherhood is a part of you—not the end of you.

Yes, you've carried pain.
Yes, you've lost parts of yourself.
But you are still here.
And you deserve to be poured into just as deeply as you pour into everyone else.

You don't need permission to come home to yourself.

Reflection 2
Journal Prompts

"You were a woman first — worthy, whole, and powerful beyond what the world asked of you"

When you think of the version of yourself, before life
asked you to carry so much...
what do you remember about her?

_____

_____

_____

_____

_____

_____

_____

_____

_____

_____

Your healing, your story, your voice-its safe here

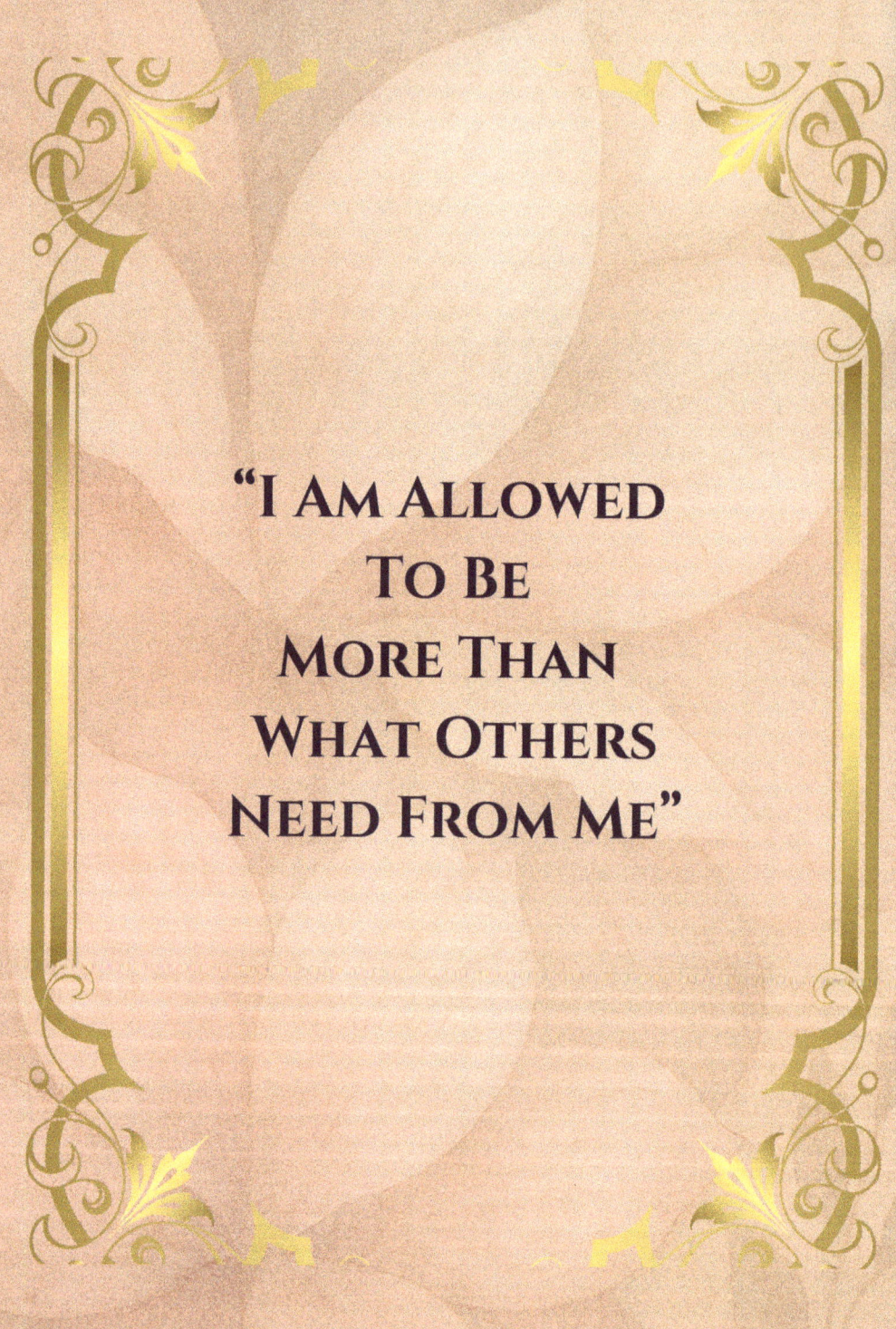

"I Am Allowed
To Be
More Than
What Others
Need From Me"

Reflection 2
Journal Prompts

*"You are more than who they needed you to be
— you are still who you were meant to be."*

Where do you feel most disconnected from the woman you used to be? Where can you begin to bridge that gap?

_____

_____

_____

_____

_____

_____

_____

_____

_____

_____

_____

_____

Your healing, your story, your voice–its safe here

Reflection 2
Journal Prompts

"Motherhood shaped you. It didn't erase you."

If you could speak to the woman you were before motherhood, grief, or pain — what would you tell her?

_____

_____

_____

_____

_____

_____

_____

_____

_____

_____

_____

_____

Your healing, your story, your voice–its safe here

✦ DAILY CHECK-IN ✦

A gentle moment to notice how you're feeling - no judgment, just awareness.

Today, I feel...

_____

_____

_____

In my body, I notice...

_____

_____

_____

A small way I can offer myself love today...

_____

_____

_____

Your healing, your story, your voice–its safe here

Reflection 3 (part 1)

"Grieving in the Quiet"

I was my father's only child. His daughter. In his words, "the love of his life". It was always him and I against the world.

You could say I was his heart walking outside his body.

Our relationship wasn't always easy. As a girl, I carried wounds I couldn't name—mistaking his distance for disinterest, his silence for not caring. For a long time, I thought I had to earn his love. Perform for it.

But as I got older, I came to see him fully—not just as my father, but as a MAN, complicated, flawed, deeply loving. I realized: I was everything to him.

Once I became an adult, we spoke every day—sometimes more than once. He never judged me. Even when I made choices he didn't agree with, he didn't shame me for my mistakes. He offered truth without cruelty. Space without distance, love without conditions.

When I told him I was pregnant at 17, he was angry—yes, disappointed —sure, but he didn't abandon me... He came back. He showed up. And when my son was born, he became the kind of grandfather I never had—steady, kind, fully present.

Even when he didn't have much, he gave everything that mattered: presence, protection, love.

He could be intense, even overbearing, but never cruel, and never unkind. His love had edges, but never thorns. It was fierce because he wanted to shield me from a world he knew could be brutal.

He was my best friend. My home. My anchor.
And I never imagined living a life where he wasn't just a phone call away.

Reflection 3 (part 1)
Journal Prompts

"The hardest part isn't the goodbye — it's learning to live with the silence they leave behind."

How have you been carrying your grief — in silence, in strength, in survival?

_____

_____

_____

_____

_____

_____

_____

_____

_____

_____

_____

_____

_____

Reflection 3 (part 1)
Journal Prompts

"Grief teaches you that love never truly leaves — it transforms, it lingers, it stays."

In what ways did their love, even imperfectly, shape who you are today?

_____

_____

_____

_____

_____

_____

_____

_____

_____

_____

_____

_____

_____

Your healing, your story, your voice–its safe here

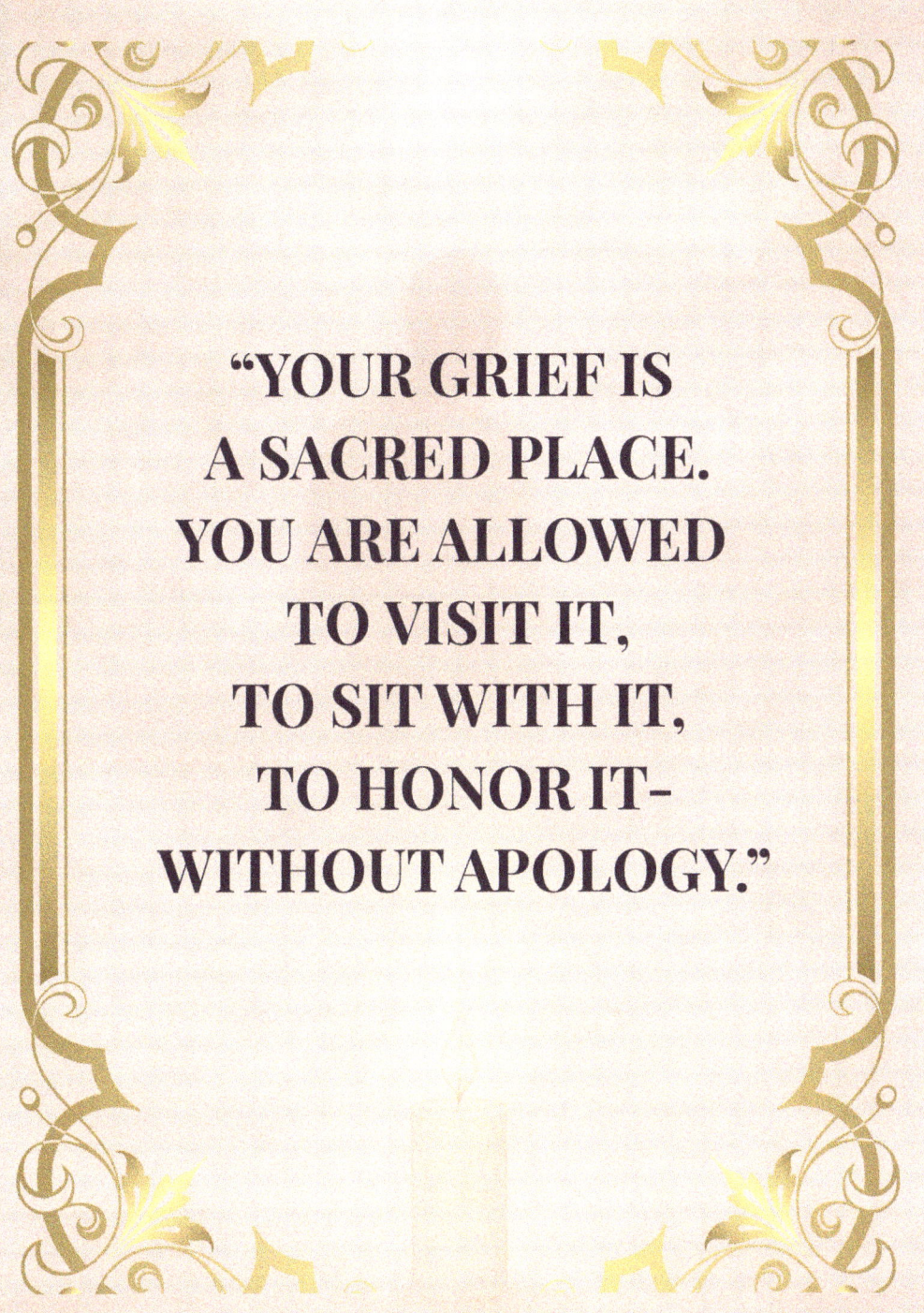

"YOUR GRIEF IS
A SACRED PLACE.
YOU ARE ALLOWED
TO VISIT IT,
TO SIT WITH IT,
TO HONOR IT-
WITHOUT APOLOGY."

Reflection 3 (part 1)
Journal Prompts

*"Some days, I still reach for the phone. Other days,
I just sit with the ache. Both are love."*

What parts of you feel lost without them — and what
parts of you are slowly learning to keep going?

_____

_____

_____

_____

_____

_____

_____

_____

_____

_____

_____

_____

Your healing, your story, your voice–its safe here

55

Reflection 3 (part 2)

"Grieving in the Quiet"

I remember the day my father died like it was yesterday.

It was a week after my birthday, on a Monday, and by 3:30 p.m, I realized he hadn't called yet—which was unlike him. He always called after work. I tried not to spiral as I called him—once, then again, and one last time. No answer. I left a few messages, but something in me knew. Something was really wrong.

I reached out to my uncle. Spoke to my aunt while he sent my cousin to check on him.
And just like that—my whole world changed.

He was gone.
A heart attack. Alone in his apartment. Lying on his recliner.

My best friend. My anchor. The only person who saw me—all of me— was suddenly... GONE.

My body shifted into survival mode, but my soul... It shattered.
I dropped to the floor, sobbing. I called people just to say his name out loud—needing to speak it, needing to make it real.
But nothing made it real.

I was numb. I was hollow.
I was searching for something to hold onto, but everything had slipped through my fingers.

And then, I saw him in the casket.

He looked peaceful—but it wasn't him. His body was there, but
everything that made him, him was missing. His warmth. His laugh.
His voice. His spirit.

Over 200 people came to his funeral.
And I had never felt so alone.

I smiled, I nodded, I thanked everyone,
and inside, I was unraveling. My body was present, but my mind
wasn't. I was somewhere else—caught between shock and sorrow
Replaying every moment, every unanswered call, every what-if.

There was no space to fall apart.
So I didn't.

The next day I went back home. Back to being a mother. Back to being
a partner. Back to life—as if everything hadn't just collapsed.

And just days after his funeral, I found out I was pregnant.

I was carrying life—while something sacred inside me had just died.
The weight of that truth nearly crushed me. I didn't know how to hold
joy and grief in the same hands.
So I didn't.
I kept moving. For my kids. For the man I loved. For everyone but me.

I grieved in bathrooms.
In five-minute breaks.
While I sat in the car alone, after grocery shopping.
In the silence.

I was expected to keep going. To stay strong. To smile.
But I was so tired.

I needed someone to hold me and say, "I see you, I'm here, you don't have to be okay".
But that moment never came.
Not from the one I needed most.

I buried it deeper.
I smiled louder.
I slowly disappeared behind my own strength.

But here's what I'm learning now:

I am allowed to grieve.
I am allowed to cry. To miss him. To say his name out loud.
My grief doesn't need to be justified—it is sacred.
It's a reflection of the love that still lives inside me.

I talk to him.
I eat the food he loved.
I share his stories with my children.
And when people ask how I'm doing, I tell the truth—because I owe myself that.

Just because I've had to be strong my whole life doesn't mean I can't be soft.
Grief doesn't make me weak.
It makes me human.

I still want to make him proud.
And I believe he's watching me become the woman he always knew I could be.

Reflection 3 (part 2)
Journal Prompts

"Some grief lives in the quiet moments — the spaces no one else notices but you."

If you let yourself speak your grief out loud, what truth would you say without apology?

_____

_____

_____

_____

_____

_____

_____

_____

_____

_____

_____

_____

Your healing, your story, your voice-its safe here

Reflection 3 (part 2)
Journal Prompts

"You learned how to carry life and loss at the same time — no one taught you, but you survived it."

What small reminder can you give yourself today that grief and love coexist?

_____

_____

_____

_____

_____

_____

_____

_____

_____

_____

_____

"THERE IS NO RIGHT WAY TO GRIEVE- THERE IS ONLY MY WAY."

Reflection 3 (part 2)
Journal Prompts

"The world expected you to be strong. But all you wanted was to be held."

What does it mean for you to hold both grief and hope at the same time?

_____

_____

_____

_____

_____

_____

_____

_____

_____

_____

_____

_____

Your healing, your story, your voice–its safe here

DAILY CHECK-IN

For the days grief feels heavy

How Am I Arriving To This Moment?

- ☐ Exhausted
- ☐ Holding it together
- ☐ Soft
- ☐ Overwhelmed
- ☐ Quietly Strong

- ☐ Numb
- ☐ Overstimulated
- ☐ Empty
- ☐ Other:_____

One Word That Descries My Heart Right Now?

_____

What My Body Needs Most Right Today?

- ☐ Rest
- ☐ Nourishment
- ☐ Comfort
- ☐ To just breathe
- ☐ A hug

- ☐ Space to cry
- ☐ Stillness
- ☐ Movement
- ☐ Other:_____

A Gentle Reminder I Need Today?

_____

One Loving Thing I Can Do For Myself Today:

_____

Your healing, your story, your voice–its safe here

Reflection 4

"The Day I Let Go of the Fantasy and Faced the Truth"

It didn't break me. It woke me up

He came into my life during one of my most vulnerable seasons. I was exhausted, terrified for my son's health, overwhelmed, and alone. My oldest was in the hospital, my second was bouncing between homes, and I was barely holding myself together.

And then there he was—gentle, compassionate, present.
He offered me comfort when no one else could.
Food when I couldn't afford it.
A safe place to rest when I was drowning.
He made me feel seen. Heard. Held.
And in my heart, I believed maybe—just maybe—he was the answer to my prayers.

I clung to that hope. To the fantasy that he was different. That he would always be my safe place.

But time began to peel back the layers.
The kindness wavered.
The compassion sometimes turned to control.
The love I thought I had found was chipped away by criticism, tension, and misunderstanding.

I started to believe I was the problem.
I tried to change—to shrink, to mold myself into what he needed.
But it never felt like enough.

The harder I tried, the smaller I became.
The woman I once was—confident, strong, powerful—began to fade.

And one day, something in me cracked open—not with a scream, but with a quiet, undeniable truth.

It wasn't just one argument, but the weight of all the silences, all the dismissals, all the moments I swallowed my hurt.
I realized: this wasn't love—not the kind I deserve.

I deserve a love that holds space for my softness.
For my flaws.
For my humanity.
The kind of love I give so freely to others.

I was afraid—of change, of loss, of what honesty might cost me.
But staying silent meant losing me.
And I couldn't do that anymore.

So I stopped pretending.
I stopped begging to be seen.
I started seeing myself.

I still pray. I still hope.
But now, I bring my whole self to the altar—grief, strength, softness, and all.
I don't pray to be loved differently.
I pray to stay rooted in the love I'm learning to give myself.

I'm still here.
Still healing.
Still reclaiming the pieces of myself I gave away too quickly.

And I'm doing it while drawing lines I once trembled to trace—softly, firmly, with my own hand.

Real love doesn't belittle.
It doesn't silence.
It doesn't dim your light.

Real love is gentle. Honest. Safe.
And so is the love I'm learning to offer myself—whether or not he ever
fully learns to meet me there.

This isn't the end of our story.
But it is the moment I chose to rewrite my role in it—
one where I come home to myself, again and again.

Reflection 4
Journal Prompts

"The truth did not break me. It freed me. I am allowed to choose myself."

What fantasy have you been holding onto—and what truth is asking to be heard?

(You can write about a relationship, a story you've told yourself, or any illusion you've outgrown)

_____
_____
_____
_____
_____
_____
_____
_____
_____
_____
_____
_____
_____

Reflection 4
Journal Prompts

"Real love doesn't shrink you–it holds space for your softness and your strength."

What fears have kept you holding on–and how can you remind yourself that choosing you isn't selfish?

_____

_____

_____

_____

_____

_____

_____

_____

_____

_____

_____

_____

_____

Your healing, your story, your voice-its safe here

"REAL LOVE HOLDS
SPACE FOR
MY FLAWS AND MY
SOFTNESS."

Reflection 4
Journal Prompts

"Letting go of the illusion isnt weakness–it is the bravest thing you will ever do."

Being completely honest, what parts of you have you lost while trying to be enough for someone else?

_____

_____

_____

_____

_____

_____

_____

_____

_____

_____

_____

_____

_____

_____

Your healing, your story, your voice–its safe here

Reflection 5

"Breaking the cycle by Becoming the Mother I Needed."

The work starts with me—and it changes everything after me

I've had to learn how to be the mother I needed while still healing the little girl inside me—the one who was left feeling unseen, unheard, and unloved far too often.

I love my mother, but the truth is, she didn't always know how to love her children the way we needed. I've come to understand her pain—how much of it came from wounds she never had the tools to heal. That doesn't erase what I went through.

Growing up, I longed to hear "I love you" more often. I wanted to feel celebrated, encouraged to be myself, free to be a child. Instead, I became responsible for things no child should carry—cooking, cleaning, raising my younger siblings, holding the weight of my parents' anger, their chaos, their hurt.

Don't get me wrong—it didn't start out that way. We had some good times, but there were many, many bad times.

I wasn't allowed to question, to speak freely, or simply be. I tiptoed through childhood—overcompensating, cleaning more, trying harder —just to feel safe.

I carried that pain with me for years.

Now, as I raise my own children, I see the echoes. The tender places where the cycle tries to creep back in. The moments when I almost lost myself in exhaustion, mental health struggles, and being overwhelmed.

But I refuse to hand those wounds down to my children.

I want my kids to see a mother who shows up with love, respect, and honesty. I want them to know they are seen, they are heard, and they matter. I tell them I love them every chance I get. I give them the space to be kids—to laugh, to play, to make mistakes without fear of rejection or punishment.

It's not easy. The hardest part of breaking the cycle is facing my own fear—fear that I'll repeat the past, that my struggles will spill over onto them. Some days I feel like I'm failing. Like I'm barely holding it all together.

But I keep choosing to show up. I remind myself that needing space doesn't make me a bad mother—it makes me human. I give myself grace. I meet their love with my own, even when I feel stretched thin. Even when my heart is heavy.

To become the mother I needed, I first had to give myself what I never had—permission to rest, to feel, to heal.

My children saved me in ways they'll never fully understand. They brought me back to life when I felt lost. They gave me a reason to keep going. Watching them laugh, play, and thrive brings healing to the little girl inside me who never got to just be.

Breaking the cycle is hard. But it's worth it. I'm not just doing this for them—I'm doing it for me, too.

I want my children to know:
You are worthy of love, just as you are.
You are not a burden.
Your feelings are valid.
You are enough.

And you are the reason I'm healing—the reason I wake up every day
determined to change the story for the generations to come.

The cycle ends with me.
And what comes next is love, peace, and healing

Reflection 5
Journal Prompts

"It's hard to become what you never had — but your doing it anyway."

What parts of your up bringing do you want to break free from — and what parts do you want to heal, not repeat?

_____

_____

_____

_____

_____

_____

_____

_____

_____

_____

_____

_____

Your healing, your story, your voice–its safe here

Reflection 5
Journal Prompts

"The work starts with you—and it will change everything after."

How have you been carrying pain that never belonged to you — and how can you begin to set it down?

_____

_____

_____

_____

_____

_____

_____

_____

_____

_____

_____

_____

_____

Your healing, your story, your voice–its safe here

"I DESERVE
THE GRACE
I SO EASILY
GIVE TO OTHERS."

Reflection 5
journal Prompts

"You are not who hurt you. You are who you choose to become."

What fears still whisper that you'll repeat the past — and how can you remind yourself that your rewriting it?

_____

_____

_____

_____

_____

_____

_____

_____

_____

_____

_____

_____

_____

_____

Your healing, your story, your voice–its safe here

Reflection 5
Journal Prompts

"Breaking the cycle isn't loud — it's in the quiet moments where you choose love, softness, and grace — even when it's hard."

What message do you want your children - and your younger self-to believe about love, worth, and safety?

_____

_____

_____

_____

_____

_____

_____

_____

_____

_____

_____

_____

Your healing, your story, your voice–its safe here

Reflection 5
Journal Prompts

"The cycle ends with you—because you chose to love youself enough to begin again. "

How can you give yourself grace on the hard days, knowing breaking the cycle is messy but worth it?

_____

_____

_____

_____

_____

_____

_____

_____

_____

_____

_____

_____

_____

_____

Your healing, your story, your voice–its safe here

✦ DAILY CHECK-IN ✦

For The Woman Breaking Cycles

How Am I Arriving To This Moment?

☐ Exhausted but present
☐ Overwhelmed   ☐ Graciously
☐ Quietly proud   ☐ Other:_____
☐ Holding space for myself
☐ Hesitant

One Word That Descrices My Heart Today:

☐ Hopeful   ☐ Guarded
☐ Heavy   ☐ Steady
☐ Numb   ☐ Holding to much
☐ At peace(for now)   ☐ Other:_____
☐ resilient

What Is One Loving Thing I Can Do For Myself Today?

_____

Your healing, your story, your voice–its safe here

Reflection 6
"I Choose Me, Even When It's Hard"

Because choosing me is choosing peace, freedom, and the life I deserve.

Choosing myself hasn't always come naturally. In fact, at times, it felt unfamiliar—uncomfortable. Almost wrong. For so long, I didn't know what it meant to put myself first. I let people cross my boundaries—sometimes I didn't even know I was allowed to have them. I silenced my truth out of fear: fear of being too much, fear of being left, fear of making others uncomfortable.

For most of my life, I gave myself away in pieces just to feel needed. I walked on eggshells. I swallowed my voice. I kept the peace at the cost of my own peace. Behind the strong exterior—the woman who holds it all together—was someone aching to feel seen. To feel heard. To feel like enough.

But something has shifted. Maybe it's the grief. Maybe it's becoming a mother all over again. Maybe it's the accumulation of all the moments I betrayed myself to protect someone else's comfort.

Whatever it is, I've started listening to the quiet voice inside that says: You matter, too.

Now I'm practicing, one small act at a time. I'm learning that my needs are valid. That my voice is not too loud. That my softness is not weakness—it's strength.

It hasn't been easy. The fear still shows up—the fear of disappointing others, of disrupting harmony, of asking for more. But I've realized: fear isn't the truth. It's just a shadow of the old me—the me who thought love had to be earned through self-sacrifice.

These days, choosing myself looks simple:
Drinking my coffee while it's still hot.
Washing my face even when I'm exhausted.
Sitting in prayer—not asking for strength to keep surviving, but for permission to start living.

There was a time I hoped someone would save me. That love would feel like safety. That someone else would see my pain and pull me from it. The truth is, I had to learn to see myself first. To honor myself. To rescue myself.

My dad's no longer here to remind me of who I am. And I've accepted that no one is coming to save me.
So I'm becoming the one who saves herself.

I'm still learning.
Learning that rest is not laziness.
That "no" is a full sentence.
That I don't have to explain my needs or justify my softness.

I used to think choosing myself meant giving up on love. But now I see—it's the only way to experience real love. The kind that holds space for all of me, not just the parts that are easy to love.

I think often of the phoenix—how it breaks, burns, turns to ash... and rises.
Not in spite of the fire, but because of it.

I've walked through my own flames.
I've lost parts of myself I thought I needed to survive.
But I'm still here. Still rising.

This is my rebirth.
This time, I'm choosing me.

Reflection 6
Journal Prompts

"I won't apologize for the space I take up anymore."

What fears rise up when you try to put yourself first —
and where do those fears really come from?

_____

_____

_____

_____

_____

_____

_____

_____

_____

_____

_____

_____

_____

Your healing, your story, your voice-its safe here

Reflection 6
journal Prompts

"Choosing yourself may be uncomfortable–but it made you impossible to ignore."

What boundaries have you been afraid to set — and what would it feel like to honor them anyway?

_____

_____

_____

_____

_____

_____

_____

_____

_____

_____

_____

_____

Your healing, your story, your voice–its safe here

Reflection 6
Journal Prompts

"It's okay to say no. It's okay to need rest. It's okay to choose yourself."

In what ways have you learned to abandon yourself to avoid being "too much" or "not enough"?

_____

_____

_____

_____

_____

_____

_____

_____

_____

_____

_____

_____

_____

_____

Your healing, your story, your voice-its safe here

"I RISE FOR MYSELF— FIERCELY, GENTLY, UNAPOLOGETICALLY."

Reflection 6
Journal Prompts

"Before I was a mother, a partner, or a caretaker–I was a woman. And I still am."

When was the last time you truly showed up for yourself, even in a small, quiet way?

_____

_____

_____

_____

_____

_____

_____

_____

_____

_____

_____

_____

Your healing, your story, your voice–its safe here

Reflection 6
Journal Prompts

"You've carried everyone else for so long — it's time to carry you now."

What does choosing yourself actually look like — not perfectly, but realistically, in your daily life?

_____

_____

_____

_____

_____

_____

_____

_____

_____

_____

_____

_____

Your healing, your story, your voice–its safe here

Reflection 7

"The Quiet Work of Becoming"

Healing isn't loud. It's daily, slow, and sacred. But it's happening.

For so long, I didn't think about what becoming the woman I wanted to be would even look like. I was stuck in survival mode—moving, doing, and coping. I thought healing would just happen one day. That being strong was enough. The truth is, I was stuck. Stuck in the same cycles and patterns I learned as a child.

My strength? It used to be loud—so loud it echoed off the walls. It wasn't real strength. It was a mask. A performance. I wore it to hide how lost I felt—how small I made myself just to avoid being a burden. I thought being healed was something others could clearly see. That it was supposed to be obvious. That it was supposed to be loud.

But I've learned... real healing is quiet.
Becoming is quiet.

The loudness was a lie—a trick to convince myself I was okay.

Now, the work I'm doing? Most people don't even see it. I do it for me —not for their approval. It's in the smallest moments: the stillness of my breath, the quiet sip of coffee before the day begins, brushing my teeth, brushing my hair, sitting outside and letting the sun touch my face.

These moments aren't loud. They aren't dramatic.
They are sacred.
And they matter.

I no longer crave validation from others. I no longer shape myself to meet everyone's expectations. I've stopped abandoning myself to make others comfortable.

I pray every day. I speak truth over myself. I give myself permission to rest, to slow down, to feel what I'm feeling without judgment. I've learned to celebrate the small wins—the tiny acts of self-love most people overlook.

And on the hard days, I give myself grace. If all I can do is breathe, pray, and exist—that's enough.
Because every small moment I choose myself, I grow. I rise.

Patience, grace, softness... those aren't just things I give to others anymore. I've finally realized I deserve them as well. I'm learning to love myself fully—the good and the messy, the beautiful and the broken parts.
They're all me.
They're all worthy of love.

If I could speak to the woman who feels stuck, I'd tell her:

You are not stuck.
You are not too much.
You are not less than.

You are everything you've ever needed—and more.
You didn't lose the woman you were meant to be.
She's still in there, waiting to rise. Waiting to be seen.

You just have to be willing to show up for yourself.
To water yourself, even when the world feels heavy.
Even when no one else notices.

Becoming isn't loud.
It's quiet.
It's daily.
It's sacred.
And it's happening—one breath at a time.

Reflection 7
Journal Prompts

"You don't owe the world your struggle, your time, or your voice — you only owe yourself grace."

What version of you have you been quietly holding onto — the woman your afraid to fully become?

Your healing, your story, your voice–its safe here

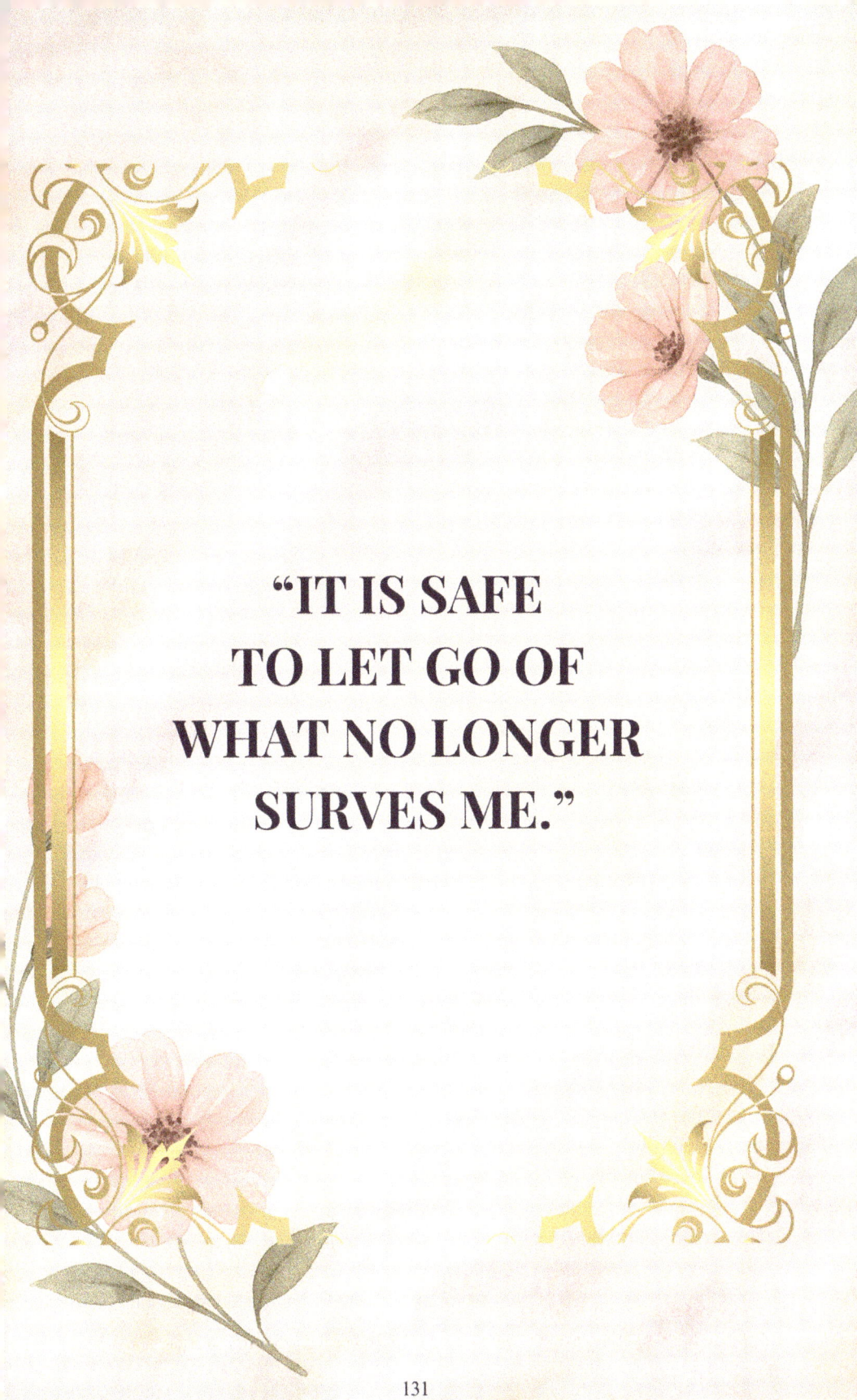

"IT IS SAFE
TO LET GO OF
WHAT NO LONGER
SURVES ME."

Reflection 7
Journal Prompts

"Your healing doesn't have to be seen to be real. It's happening — one quiet moment at a time."

What small moments — even ones no one noticed — have reminded you
that your still here, still growing?

Your healing, your story, your voice-its safe here

Reflection 7
Journal Prompts

"I no longer crave validation — I crave peace. And that's enough."

What part of your daily routine could you turn into a sacred act of self - love?

_____

_____

_____

_____

_____

_____

_____

_____

_____

_____

_____

_____

_____

Your healing, your story, your voice-its safe here

✦ DAILY CHECK-IN: ✦

For The Woman Still Becoming

How Am I Arriving To This Moment?

☐ Exhausted but present
☐ Overwhelmed
☐ Quietly proud
☐ Holding space for myself
☐ Hesitant

☐ Graciously
☐ Other:_____

One Word That Descries My Heart Today:

☐ Hopeful
☐ Heavy
☐ Numb
☐ At peace(for now)
☐ resilient

☐ Guarded
☐ Steady
☐ Holding to much
☐ Other:_____

What Is One Loving Thing I Can Do For Myself Today?

_____

Your healing, your story, your voice–its safe here

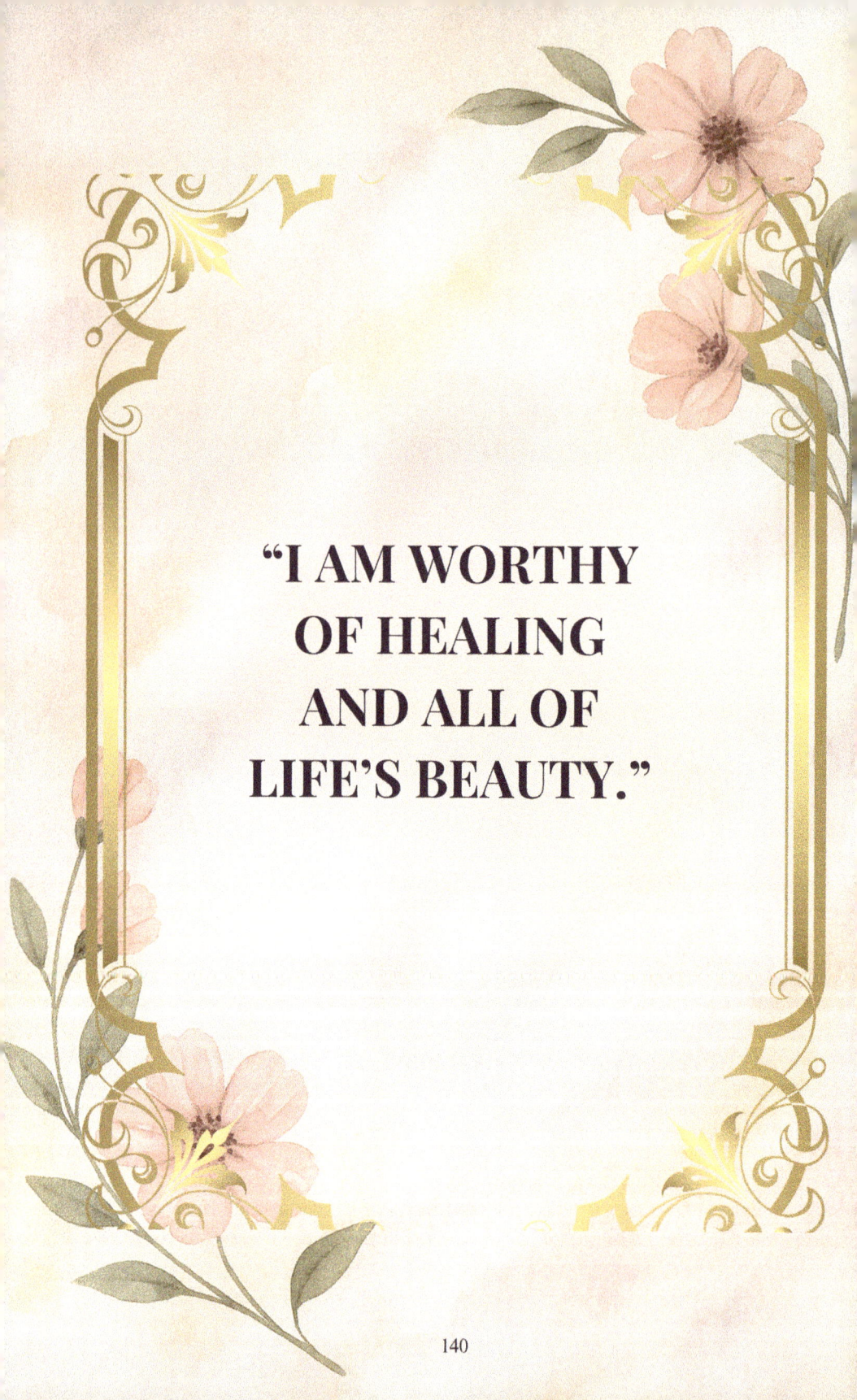

"I AM WORTHY
OF HEALING
AND ALL OF
LIFE'S BEAUTY."

Reflection 7
Journal Prompts

""Becoming yourself again isn't dramatic — it's daily, slow, and sacred."

In the moments when no one is watching, how do you show yourself love — even in small, messy ways?

_____
_____
_____
_____
_____
_____
_____
_____
_____
_____
_____
_____
_____

Your healing, your story, your voice-its safe here

Reflection 7
Journal Prompts

*"You didn't lose the woman you were meant to be —
she's still here, quietly waiting to rise."*

If you believed becoming wasn't about perfection, but
about softness, how would you treat yourself today?

Your healing, your story, your voice-its safe here

Reflection 7
Journal Prompts

"The pieces you doubt are often the ones that carry the most light."

What parts of you still feels unworthy of becoming —
and how can you remind yourself she's allowed to rise?

Your healing, your story, your voice–its safe here

Reflection 8
"Rising from the ashrs"

The fire didn't break me. It became the reason I rose.

There have been so many fires in my life, I don't even know where to start.

It began when I was young—a moment that changed everything. I didn't know how to cope, and no one showed me how. I felt lost, confused, alone. I was sent away to a new place, far from everything familiar. And even though I still lived with family, they couldn't see what I was carrying. Everyone assumed I was strong. That I'd be okay, but inside, I was quietly burning.

At 18, I became a mother—raising a child alone, working, trying to hold it all together, but life didn't slow down. My son's health struggles began, and I found myself in hospital rooms, overwhelmed by fear. I didn't know if he would be okay. I carried that fear silently.

I turned to unhealthy coping just to survive. I was drowning, unsure of how to face the weight of it all.

And still, the fires came.

My son's condition worsened. I had another child to care for. I juggled hospitals, exhaustion, and guilt—guilt for not being everywhere at once. Guilt for feeling overwhelmed.

Then came a relationship I thought would be safe, but it wasn't.
Bit by bit, I lost myself—my confidence, my voice, my sense of worth...
chipped away.

And then... I lost my dad.
 My anchor, my rock. The only man who truly saw me.

That was my breaking point.

I shattered. I stayed in a place that drained me. I had another baby. I
showed up for my family, but I couldn't find myself. I was burnt out. I
disconnected from my joy, my identity, and my spirit.

The woman in the mirror? I didn't recognize her.
My body was here, but my soul was gone.

I couldn't fall any lower.

But one day... I realized I was still here.
Still breathing.
Still surviving.

Life was moving forward, and I couldn't stay stuck.
My kids were growing, learning, living—and I wanted to live, too.

I've survived every fire life has thrown at me.
Moments that should have broken me—didn't.
I'm still standing.

There is so much strength in me.
So much beauty that never left—only got buried beneath the ashes.

The fires didn't destroy me.
They taught me how to rise.

Do I still fear things? Of course.
I fear abandonment, judgment, and failure. I've doubted myself.
I've let others define my worth. I've looked outside myself for
approval.
I'm done with that now.

I've learned the only voice that matters is mine.
I'm learning to be me—unapologetically.
To set boundaries.
To speak up.
To choose myself.

Even when it's hard.
Even when it's quiet.

I still have fears.
But I rise anyway.

I'm not just surviving anymore—
I'm choosing to live.

My kids deserve to see that.
And so do I.

I'm reclaiming my power.
I'm honoring my grief.
I'm giving myself permission to rest, to take up space, to heal.

And slowly, I feel my confidence returning.

I know I can rise above what I've been through—
and come out softer, stronger, wiser.

I'm learning to give myself the same love
I've always poured into others.

And to you, reading this:
If you're just surviving right now—
That's okay.

But hear me:
You were meant to live, not just survive.

Your past does not define you.
You are worthy of joy, of peace,
of becoming the woman you've always dreamed of being.

Even if you're a mother.
A partner.
A caregiver—

You're still a woman.

And you can still rise.

Start small.
One breath at a time.

In the quiet moments, you'll feel her—
the woman you were always meant to be—
rising.

It's not easy.
I'm still figuring it out, too.

But I promise you—it's worth it.

Give yourself grace.
Be patient.
Keep going.

The fire didn't break me.
It's why I rise.

Reflection 8
Journal Prompts

"You burned, you broke, you may have even disappeared — but you're still standing."

What parts of you feel lost, broken, or buried — and what small steps can you take to begin rising again?

_____

_____

_____

_____

_____

_____

_____

_____

_____

_____

_____

_____

_____

_____

Your healing, your story, your voice–its safe here

Reflection 8
Journal Prompts

"I thought the fire ended me — but it awakened the woman I was always meant to be."

What fires have you walked through that you thought would destroy you — but didn't?

_____

_____

_____

_____

_____

_____

_____

_____

_____

_____

_____

_____

_____

_____

Your healing, your story, your voice–its safe here

Reflection 8
Journal Prompts

"You can rise while afraid. You can rise while grieving. You can in rise anyway.

How have you allowed fear, exhaustion, or grief to silence your worth — and how can you reclaim your voice?

_____
_____
_____
_____
_____
_____
_____
_____
_____
_____
_____
_____
_____

Your healing, your story, your voice-its safe here

"I AM RECLAIMING
MY PEACE,
ONE STEP AT
A TIME."

Reflection 8
Journal Prompts

*"I've walked through fires no one saw —
and I'm still here."*

What strength did the fire reveal in you that you didn't
know you carried?

_____

_____

_____

_____

_____

_____

_____

_____

_____

_____

_____

_____

_____

Your healing, your story, your voice-its safe here

Reflection 8
Journal Prompts

"I thought I had to survive in silence–but even in the ashes, my soul was learning how to rise."

How have you measured your worth by your ability to carry pain — and how can you redefine your worth with softness and grace?

_____

_____

_____

_____

_____

_____

_____

_____

_____

_____

_____

_____

_____

Reflection 8
Journal Prompts

"From every flame, I gathered light. From every fall, I rose stronger, wiser, more myself."

What has the fire taught you—and how are you ready to rise?

_____

_____

_____

_____

_____

_____

_____

_____

_____

_____

_____

_____

_____

Your healing, your story, your voice–its safe here

" AND STILL,
I RISE—
ONE BREATH
AT A TIME."

✦ DAILY CHECK-IN ✦

Right Now, I Feel:

☐ Tender	☐ Scared	
☐ Hopeful	☐ Joyful	
☐ Lost	☐ Other: _____	
☐ Empty		
☐ Uncertain		

A gentle affirmation I need today:

_____

_____

One peaceful moment I can savor:

_____

_____

What does journaling offer me in this moment?

_____

_____

Your healing, your story, your voice–its safe here

Reflection 9

"Becoming, Still"

I've had more good days than bad lately.

That might seem small to someone else—but for me, it's everything. It means the grief isn't as heavy. The sadness doesn't sit on my chest the way it used to. I still cry sometimes—usually in the bathroom, when no one's looking—but it's not every day anymore. That's a win.

I've stuck to my routines—even on the days I'm running on fumes. I get up. I wash my face. I brush my teeth. I show up for myself in the smallest ways—even when no one's watching. And when I don't have the strength? I give myself grace. I don't spiral in guilt. I just try again tomorrow.

My thoughts have started to shift as well. I'm not constantly stuck in worst-case scenarios. I'm more aware of what I do have. I pray every day. I give thanks. Even when it's uncomfortable, I speak up. I say how I feel. That alone is healing.

I'm getting outside more with my kids. It's not easy—pushing a wheelchair with a baby on my chest takes strength most people will never understand. But I do it. I show up. I make the effort, because I want them to remember a mother who tried. Not one who was perfect —but one who kept showing up.

And the truth is... I am feeling better. Not fixed. Not finished, but lighter. More aware. More present.

I know I still have a lot of work to do. I've made mistakes. I've hurt my partner, too. I'm not here pretending to be the hero of every chapter. I'm just here—choosing to do the work. To grow. To unlearn. To apologize when I need to, and to become someone I'm proud of.

I'm doing this for my children, for myself, and for my partner.
Because if I'm going to keep trying to build something, I want to do it with a whole heart. Not one buried in pain and silence.

This is what becoming looks like—
not a perfect transformation—
but a quiet, steady return.
To truth. To softness. To strength.
And I'll keep rising—imperfect, wholehearted, and unafraid to begin again.

Some days I rise with strength. Some days, I simply breathe through it.
But either way—I'm still becoming.

And that matters.

A Glimpse Into My World

A Sacred Pause — Final Reflection

You've made it this far — that alone is powerful.

Before you rise into the next chapter of your becoming, these last few prompts are here to help you anchor everything you've uncovered.

This isn't the end — it's a quiet pause. A space to honor how far you've come... to soften... to stand taller... to remember the woman you've always been is still in there, waiting to be seen.

Take your time. Breathe through these final reflections.
There's no rush — only the sacred work of choosing yourself.

You're still becoming — and you've never been more ready.

Final Reflection Prompts

"Even in the quiet, I've grown."

How do you feel now, compared to when you first opened these pages?

_____

_____

_____

_____

_____

_____

_____

_____

_____

_____

_____

_____

_____

_____

Your healing, your story, your voice–its safe here

Final Reflection Prompts

"You're story is not a burden — it's proof of your strength."

What part of your story feels softer, more seen, or more understood after these pages?

_____

_____

_____

_____

_____

_____

_____

_____

_____

_____

_____

_____

Your healing, your story, your voice-its safe here

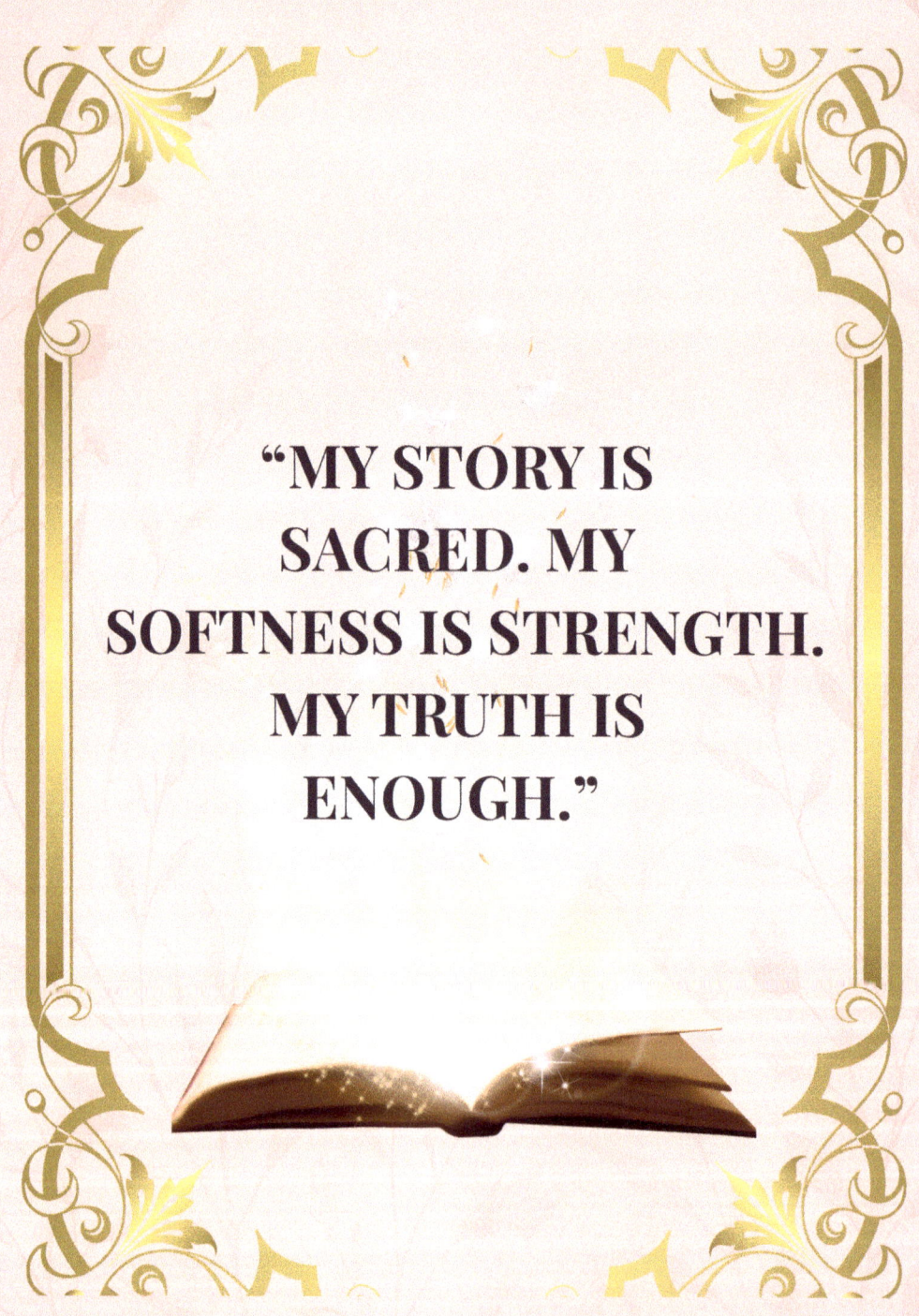

"MY STORY IS
SACRED. MY
SOFTNESS IS STRENGTH.
MY TRUTH IS
ENOUGH."

Final Reflection Prompts

"Even on the hard days, you're still becoming."

What is one truth you want to carry with you on the hard days?

_____

_____

_____

_____

_____

_____

_____

_____

_____

_____

_____

_____

A Sacred Pause — Your Final Reflection Prompts

"You know the way back to yourself."

When you forget you're worth or feel lost, how can you gently guide myself back home?

_____

_____

_____

_____

_____

_____

_____

_____

_____

_____

_____

Your healing, your story, your voice-its safe here

Final Reflection Prompts

"Choose yourself — gently, boldly,, without apology."

What does choosing yourself look like from this moment forward — not perfectly, but honestly?

_____

_____

_____

_____

_____

_____

_____

_____

_____

_____

_____

_____

Your healing, your story, your voice-its safe here

You Are Still Becoming–
Don't Forget Her

Dear Beautiful Soul,

You've walked through fire.
You've carried the weight of grief.
You've questioned your worth.
You've survived days that should've broken you — and yet... here you are.

You're still breathing.
You're still becoming.
You're still rising.

This journal wasn't meant to fix you — because you were never broken.
It was meant to remind you: your healing is sacred.
Your grief is holy ground.
Your rising? That's your birthright.

You weren't sent here to only survive, love — you were sent to live.
To reclaim the pieces of yourself that got lost beneath the weight of life, motherhood, loss, pain, and expectations.

The woman within you — the soft one, the fierce one, the one who knows her worth — she was never gone.
She was buried beneath survival. Beneath silence. Beneath exhaustion.

But not anymore.

You're not walking out of this journal the same.
You're walking out softer, yes — but stronger. Louder. Braver.
Grounded.

The world may not understand your quiet strength. Let them
wonder.
The world may not celebrate your small healing. Celebrate yourself
anyway.
The world may never see the fires you've walked through.
But God did — and He is still holding you in His arms.

So rise — in your own time, in your own way, with your own sacred
grace.
The ashes you thought would consume you?
They're the foundation you're building on now.

This isn't your ending — this is your awakening.
Breathe. Take up space. Speak softly. Love fiercely. Rise fully.

With love, power, and divine belief in your becoming,

Erika
A Woman Who Sees You

When It Feels Too Heavy

If at any point this journal opened something tender — something raw or buried — I want you to know this:

You don't have to hold it all on your own.

These pages are a beginning, not a solution.
Sometimes we need someone to hold space for us — outside of these lines, outside of our own strength.

If you ever find yourself needing more support, here are places that offer real help, without judgment:

———

🌙 988 Suicide & Crisis Lifeline
For when you feel overwhelmed or alone
Call or text 988 | 988lifeline.org

Postpartum Support International
For mothers navigating pregnancy, postpartum, or burnout
Call or text 1-800-944-4773 | postpartum.net

🔴 National Domestic Violence Hotline
If you're in a relationship that feels unsafe or depleting
Call 1-800-799-7233 | Text "START" to 88788 | thehotline.org

📱 Crisis Text Line
When you need someone to talk to, anytime
Text "HOME" to 741741 | crisistextline.org

Asking for support doesn't make you weak — it means you're still fighting for yourself.
And that is a quiet, holy kind of power.

You Are Not Alone.

SHE IS MORE CO.

Dedication

I want to take a moment to dedicate this journal to my father — your loss shattered me in more ways than I can count. But the love I know you carried for me — the way you saw me, believed in me — it's what gave me the strength to start picking up the pieces and slowly, quietly, becoming whole again.

To my children — you are the reason I rise every day. You are the reason I started choosing myself, the reason I fight so hard to heal, to grow, to become the woman I know I'm meant to be. You three deserve the very best of me. You are my reason, my hope, and why I still stand today. Mommy loves you more than words will ever be able to hold.

To the woman holding these pages, unraveling quietly, rising softly — this is your space. To grieve. To breathe. To remember: You've never been lost — only becoming and You Are Not Alone!

And above all, I dedicate this to God — for without Him, none of this would be possible. It is His grace that carried me through the darkest seasons. His love that never let me fall too far. His quiet whisper that reminded me I was never alone — and that my healing could become a light for others. He is the reason I rise, the reason I love, and the reason I'm here sharing this space with you now.

In Loving Memory of my dad
Juan Santiago
(Johnny Boy)
1961 - 2023

Your legacy lives on through us